Images of a Marriage

A Collection of Poems, Photographs & Stories
Celebrating the Seasons of Marriage

Sophia V. Brooks, M.S.

With Photography by
Sophia V. Brooks • Joe & Monica Cook • Steve David • J. Scott Graham
Alan Ostmann • Jennifer Pickering • Stephen A. Snider • Visio Photography

Catch the Spirit of Appalachia, Inc.
WESTERN NORTH CAROLINA

FIRST EDITION 2012

Book Layout by Amy Ammons Garza
Cover Design by Amanda Pertillor
Front Cover Photography & Illustration "After Katrina" by Sophia V. Brooks

Illustration of Author on Back Cover by Rebecca N. King
Influenced by the art and philosophies of the past and present, Rebecca King's art is centered around light and color relationships in the natural world and the emotive weight of relative natural, and formal elements.

Scripture verses used within this book are from KJV or NIV

PUBLISHER
Ammons Communications – SAN No. 8 5 1 – 0 8 8 1
Imprint: Catch the Spirit of Appalachia
29 Regal Avenue Sylva, North Carolina 28779
Phone/fax: 828/631-4587

Library of Congress Control Number: 2012950361

ISBN #978-09853728-2-8

Dedication

This book is dedicated to all the husbands and wives who have persevered in their love, honored their marriage commitments, and found the grace to endure trials and tribulations walking hand in hand toward a season of ripeness—an inspiration to us all.

Acknowledgments

How to say thank you to so many, many people, and where to start?

Perhaps I will begin with my own parents, Leonard and Susan. They brought me into this world with abundant love and celebration. My mother's joyful anticipation as she carried me, became the foundation of my trust. In a life filled with much challenge, knowing that the world is a wonderful and welcoming place, has made all the difference. I patterned my career and life's work after that of my father. His devotion to helping families and especially children grow and thrive inspired me during the many years I witnessed his tireless and generous giving.

My father's parents, Walter (a painter) and Ruth, nurtured the emerging artist of my childhood as did my mother's parents Fred and Sue. She was also a watercolor artist and a weaver. Growing up I was immersed in the beauty of the natural world; sailing on the Chesapeake Bay, swimming at Lake George and hiking in the beautiful Adirondack Mountains.

I thank the talented photographers who have captured such beauty and willingly shared their sublime images for this book. The breathless wonder and excitement of the natural world has always been and continues to be, the wind beneath my sails that carries me through life's gusts and gales. Please enjoy their inspiring work.

I hold in esteem and respect my own sons – Allen and Nathan who accompanied me on many adventures through uncharted waters to carve out their own courageous paths and explorations. Without their company the early years would have been a lonely walk.

I have learned so much about marriage and family life from so many folks during the past 30 years. They have put their trust in me and in the Creator who guides my hand and tunes my ear to his voice. I welcome and appreciate the thoughts, advice and words of wisdom from many husbands and wives. They have shared my excitement in compiling creative and sometimes humorous anecdotes to tickle your funny bone.

The couples who have shared dialogues for each season of marriage in the book have truly spoken from the heart and selflessly shared many intimate details from behind closed doors. I acknowledge their trust in this project and their trust in me. Without their courageous sharing the book would have been beautiful, but not as truthful as I wanted it to be. Where the rubber meets the road is what I wanted and what I got. So, it is what I am able to offer to you my reader.

Many friends have believed in my vision. They supported my

dream and encouraged me through the thick and thin. You know who you are and you know the opposition I encountered to bring this work to completion. You stood by my side through it all.

Thanks to Susan O., Martina, Mary D., Bill and Carol, Bob and Susan, Mike and Bette, George and Kathleen, Stephen and Bea, Father Wilbur Thomas, Hugh and Penny, Terry and Joy. So many of these folks prayed diligently for me including all the gals in the Alpha class at First Baptist Church of Asheville. Thank you Dr. Guy Sayles, pastor and guide, for believing in me and my vision for this book to be an inspiration for couples who faithfully embrace and honor their marriage covenants.

A special shout out to Deane Kells who proofed for me and used her fine skills to uncover many ellusive grammatical errors and weird spelling blunders. Thank you for the polish.

There is a diamond hidden in the rough and her name is Amanda. She has served as my typist and graphic artist. With always a willing heart and cheerful smile she creates small miracles on a daily basis from the scraps and scribbles I entrust to her capable hands. Thank you Amanda, may you always remain close to home!

My deepest appreciation goes to my publisher and friend, Amy Ammons Garza. I feel so blessed to have stumbled upon you Amy, and Catch the Spirit of Appalachia Publishing. There are no accidents in life, not when you have been praying for 20 years! Amy, you have been such a delight to work with. Thank you for your talent, your sweet spirit and your fervent voice of encouragement.

And lastly, for the stranger in the coffee shop with the red polka dot bowtie. Bob, you kept asking the same question, "Sophia, when are you going to publish your book?" Until finally, at the third time of asking, after recounting all my excuses, set backs and frustration, I gulped, swallowed hard and replied, "This year!"

Table of Contents

Introduction

Many events and social trends since World War II have put tremendous stress on the American family, and the rate of divorce has continued to soar during these past 70 years. Yet every day in the newspaper near the announcements about marriage and divorce are a few photographs of men and women in their 80s and 90s, people who endured and fought in that war and are now celebrating their golden wedding anniversary and beyond. "How do they do it?" I have often wondered. The generations of my own family have experienced so much divorce. I began to be curious. What pearls of wisdom might they have to offer younger couples? Had anyone ever talked to them about the "endurance factor" in marriage?

So, I began asking husbands and wives what had helped them preserve their marriage over the years. You will find their thoughts on the Season pages in this book, that precede each section of poetry. During my work with couples as a psychotherapist, and upon listening to family and friends, I have observed that marriages move through different seasons. It seemed natural for this book to progress in the same way.

Many couples feel isolated when they are in the midst of a painful struggle. They may be embarrassed or ashamed to talk about what is happening. Often they think the pain means it is a "bad marriage," or a "mistake" and should be terminated. They do not understand that all couples move through times of pain and stress. It is just that some are able to do it and remain together. Often they come through their "trial by fire" with a stronger and more honest union.

The poems in this book also trace the journey of a love relationship: the tears, the joy, and the laughter. Sometimes the painful struggles of marriage are so intense that neither person feels they can endure another day. These feelings, too, are captured in the poetry and in the photographs of the natural world. In the final analysis, our commitment to any challenge is not an intellectual decision, but rather a turning of the heart. Poems and pictures speak to the heart. Many people find rest and comfort in the out-of-doors. Others find excitement, adventure, and inspiration while marveling at God's creative wonder and beauty. Human love is fragile and delicate, while God's love is strong and enduring. The Creator's work proclaims this endurance and strength.

These pictures, in a symbolic way, express the hope and fear of all people regardless of age or race. They express our desire to rise above our limitations and become who we believe we can be. Indeed, in our own strength and from our limited perspective, we cannot overcome jealousies, disappointments, betrayals, and infidelities. But there is a power greater than ourselves we can embrace if we will but open our hearts. Through Divine grace we can love beyond our fears and forgive beneath our pain.

It is difficult to discuss subtle matters of the heart in all their nuance and complexity. Maybe you have already studied many self-help books on relationships. Perhaps you are still pursuing answers and searching for hope. Perhaps you are looking at these pictures and reading the poetry on your honeymoon. Whether you are young or old, this book will be an experience rather than a lesson, a breathing rather than a set of breath exercises.

Between these covers, you will find words forged deep in the souls of husbands and wives. You will hear the music of love poems and experience the beauty of God's creation in pictures of the natural world. These pictures tell the story of what it means to love someone for a lifetime. This book is a song of celebration to sooth the heart of a tired and restless world.

—*Sophia V. Brooks*

Musings on Marriage

Marriage is, of course, many things—but most of all it is two persons living together with a kind of care and gentleness that is hardly ordinary; two persons not able only to recognize their mutual need for love, but able to understand that each is a person in his or her own right. So, be cautious of the temptation to try and possess the other. Know that to have a marriage in which each of you is free to grow, in which each of you can dare to step over the edges of where you already are, requires you be sensitive to the inevitable changes in one another. You will develop a perception that is, quite simply, the ability to hear the other above the sounds of your own preoccupation with yourself.

To be truly married, to live fully together...all this is to take a chance on that rare, seemingly impossible intimacy that goes far, far beyond words. It is, in effect, daring to allow love to happen over and over again as if for the first time, allowing it to take whatever forms, whatever expressions, that give you joy and the breathless ease of satisfaction. And too, it is knowing there are no guarantees; knowing vows can come to mean different things with time, become diluted by seemingly small, sudden angers and hurts, and yet survive, become even stronger, develop new, more compelling meanings. It is simply that you will live many different lives, some together and some apart, and that sharing them, wholly and honestly, can only bring you closer.

And remember, this will be your marriage; not one defined or sanctioned by others...that the two of you will be the only ones who will ever really know the language and the depth of your togetherness, your intimacy. What others, the world out there, will see, will be only shadows, mere reflections of your life together, and not what you know it to be.

—Anonymous

Here and there does not matter
Rather, we must be still and still moving
Into another intensity
For a further union, a deeper communion.

—T.S. Eliot, adapted

To discover another human being with whom one's relationship can have a growing depth, beauty and joy is clearly a kind of miracle. Such an inner progression of love between two persons is a most marvelous thing — a thing which can almost never be found by wishing or searching for it. It is, perhaps, the most divine of all accidents . . . .

—Walpole, adapted

Apache Wedding Prayer (adapted)

Now you will feel no rain,
   for each of you will be shelter to the other.
Now you will feel no cold,
   for each of you will be warmth to the other.
Now there is no loneliness for you;
   you remain two persons,
   but now there is only one life before you.
So go now to your dwelling place
   to enter into the days of your togetherness,
And may your days be good, and long,
                              together . . .

Bea: I fell in love with Stephen's creative and unpredictable poetic side. When he came to the party where we met, he sported half a moustache. I couldn't take my eyes off him.

Stephen: I can still take you to the place where I pulled the car over from the freeway at two in the morning. I just sat there, stunned with the strangest feeling; I was in love...with Bea!

I can remember after we got married thinking, these are things she liked in me before. I am spontaneous, poetic and unboundaried. Why can't she allow me to be a bit messy and be a little more understanding of my creative response to time and money?

Bea: I couldn't know then that criticizing him was my attempt to feel cared for. He heard his mother in my voice, and when he withdrew and grew cold, I felt the deep pain of my father's distancing from me. Because we were unconscious in our reactions to one another, we spent more than a few years believing that the other woke up each morning deliberately wanting to inflict pain.

Stephen: I would welcome the fighting when it came because, in a strange way I knew it would end the pain of the deep dark mood that was like being trapped in the freezing chains of a dungeon. As hurtful as the accusations flying back and forth were, I knew I was coming out of the aloneness.

Bea: I hated his moods. They were a poison that withered the plants in our home. But, hey, I was good in my own way and could engage in the power struggle. Getting to a place of being honest with my feelings-- directly--was a turning point.

Stephen: For me a turning point came in the desert (isn't that where it happens for all the great Saints?"). Bea and I were walking and arguing at that stage of our relationship. We could go toe to toe.

But this time I had my logic constructed brilliantly. The Supreme Court would vote for my argument. Strangely, she would have none of it.

Then, it hit me (was it a thunderbolt, an Angel's right hook?)...she felt like I wasn't listening to her! She said, "Where have you been for 13 years?" That was the beginning of me holding back the brightest of my suggestions, and learning simply to validate her experience.

"Sounds like that must have really hurt, Sweetie."

Bea: The best ingredient of the recipe for success in our relationship after 20 years continues to be honoring our weekly communication date. No distractions get in the way of our sharing. The addition of expressed appreciations, no matter how hot the frustrations, is crucial.

Stephen: Just having her show up without reminding her, somehow calms a little boy within who is terrified of being unloved and abandoned.

Learning each other's love language has not been easy. For years I gave her cards and gazillions of hugs to make her day. What she really wanted was for me to make her bed.

Bea: I like the house vacuumed, the kitchen cleaned. For Stephen to ask me, 'What could I do that would be helpful?' When he asks that, I feel deeply cared for. He likes those cards and hugs. I know that's what he likes.

Stephen: Time, experiences shared with full leavenings of joy and pain, all of these fill a cup that's part of the altar from where we celebrate our marriage.

At the time of this interview, Stephen and Beatrice had been married 20 years and lived in Bend, Oregon. At the time of publication, Stephen and Beatrice are celebrating their 37th wedding anniversary.

Season of Beginning

"She is a pearl beyond price. I thank God every day for bringing her into my life."

Mr. and Mrs. E.W. Yonkers, N.Y. Married 5 years

"It's taken ten years to learn I can't change her (sometimes I still try!). I'm coming to accept our differences as the spice in our marriage."

Mr. and Mrs. P.S. Fargo, N.D. Married 10 years

"At the wedding, our pastor said, "I want to talk to you about one word which is the farthest thing from your mind right now, but will prove indispensable in the years ahead. That word is forgiveness." Mr. and Mrs. H.P. Asheville, N.C. Married 18 years

"He's my best friend. I look forward to seeing him every day and I can't imagine spending as much time with anyone else."

Mr. and Mrs. P.S. Fargo, N.D. Married 10 years

"Our Jewish heritage is a binding force in our marriage. The sacred holidays and feasts we celebrate with family and friends are filled with warmth and joy. This gift we pass on to our children with hope and promise."

Mr. and Mrs. R. B. Albany, N.Y. Married 15 years

Complementarity of energies
Waxing and waning
light on water
ripples of pleasure
smooth and rough.

Calm days and stormy days.
Nights when the shadow of your soul
holds me in music.

A tenderness beyond tenderness
trembles with the delicacy
of new growth.

Exploring the adventure of our shared path
Fresh and gleaming with handfuls of hope.
Juice running clear and pure.

Eyes open and bright,
filled with the mirror
of your love.

Love in the fullness of youth and passion.
Laying claim to the mine of who you are
and the yours of who I am.

Together against the world,
indestructible,
shouts of triumph
echo down corridors of time
to a place of ripe delight.

Testing our strength,
pitted against the challenges of time
and space.

Knowing the sweet taste of victory
we run through forests
holding hands,
laughter rising in the careless night.

"*There is a river whose streams make glad the city of God.*"
—*Psalms 46:4*

Season of Yearning
Looking Back With Babies

Let's talk about intimacy in marriage—not just sex, but that too. The rhythm of a marriage, the pace of the day, intrusions, can either build or break down the love, trust and physical connection within a marriage. Often in the beginning, chemistry is strong and the sexual connection for both partners is passionate, fun and satisfying. Ideally, intimacy in the bedroom should be a source of pleasure and bonding for husbands and wives over all the years of their marriage. Let's listen to Paul and Rebecca talk about how this has played out for them as they begin their family.

Rebecca: From our very first date I knew I was in trouble. We closed down a Taco Bell after a hike in the woods, and a Mexican restaurant the next week. It didn't matter where we were, there was always something fascinating to talk about. I loved hearing Paul's refreshing unpredictable perspective, his creative analogies, his goofy jokes. We agreed about so much when it came to faith and expectations of life. I realized how easy it was to be with him and talk to him. I'd really rather do that than any thing else! He didn't seem put off by my strong opinions, and his shining blue eyes taught me how to be a more active listener. Since I am an introvert, it was a startling discovery to find I actually preferred to be with Paul than by myself.

Paul: I remember getting up the nerve to ask Rebecca out. We hit it off and went out to eat the first night. We talked about everything. It was fun to see how much we had in common, and even cooler to see how well we complimented one another, even in conversation. Right at the end of the ride home I got up the courage to ask her out again and when she said "Sure. When?" I said … "How about tomorrow night?" I couldn't get enough. I was excited by the way her quiet manner could not hide her confidence and her intelligence. That night I went home and told my older brother I was going to marry her! I had never been so sure of any-thing in my entire life.

Rebecca: In our first few years of marriage, I was uncomfortable expressing how I really felt about areas where we had tension. I would internalize my feelings and try to guess at Paul's feelings and motivations. Somehow I felt embarrassed and ashamed about being upset with him. Luckily Paul wouldn't let me get away with my brooding mood for long. He would sit, as he gave me his full attention and gently ask me to talk about how I was feeling. I often felt confused and stuffed up as I tried to find a way to say what I was thinking.

Paul: Some of the time sitting and talking through an argument wasn't the best thing to do right in the midst of our frustration. It took me a while to realize that sometimes when we were arguing Rebecca just needed space and time to think. That was hard for me to accept because I felt like we were just giving up rather than resolving the conflict. I, being the man, wanted to "fix" it. Inevitably when I learned to give Rebecca some time after an argument we became apologetic and understanding of each other later on.

Rebecca: Conflict was an unusual experience in our young life together; we were and always have been fast friends. I felt so reassured when I did try to clear the air. Paul would always react in a way I could not pre-dict. I discovered he is not a man of clichés, but a man of deep, peceptive feeling.

If I tried to box him into a cliché, he would never stay boxed in, but would always do or say something unpredictable and unexpected. This showed me he was listening and was challenged by it. Never was he overrun by my criticism. I love this about Paul; he takes my criticism on the chin, and he is his own man.

Paul: One of the things I love most about Rebecca is the way she challenges me. She is amazing at asking just the right question to help bring out what I really want to express. I can remember when we were dating she asked me a question after I made a blanket statement about someone. "You think you're a pretty good guy. Don't you?" she said. With that statement and some conversation afterwards she opened my eyes to an arrogance I had carried inside for years without realizing it. I still think back on that conversation as a pivotal step in my life.

Rebecca: Since I first realized I was falling in love with Paul, our level of trust has continued to grow. I knew anything less than a deep, warm partnership was not what I wanted in marriage. It was so important for me to retain who I am, and to complement him. I did not want to be absorbed by him, hidden in his shadow or to overpower him. I still find him the most interesting and unpredictable, funny, playful, sunny, loyal confidante at any party. He has been my best friend for 16 years, half of my life, and each day still seems like a new discovery, a path we can explore together. We can turn a quick meal at Subway into a satisfying exchange. Our apprehension about the future and frustrations with life begin to soften as we listen and offer each other a word of encouragement, comfort and a lightening of the mood.

The transition to having babies was a lot easier than I expected. Since Paul had lost his father a year and half before we met, I sensed fathering for him was a way to recover and build on the great relationship he had with his dad. As his best friend, I knew I couldn't withhold this experience from him. Deep down I recognized it would be good for my soul as well, but I confess I did stall for a few years. I felt conflicted and afraid of losing my time and my own career aspirations.

Paul was always reassuring. He encouraged me and agreed he didn't want to lose me to Mamaland. He said he did want children, but he did not want me to birth our children until I was ready. It took me about 18 months to finally decide, "yes." The transition to parenthood was more wonderful than I had anticipated and it became our shared adventure as a couple. I discovered the deep joy of caring for our first baby boy. Waking in darkness was an easy pleasure and greeting this new soul in the quiet of night was an intimate joy. Paul, to this day, always comes home smiling, eager to soak up time with our children and me. I so enjoy seeing him interact with our children. It makes me love them all so much more.

Paul: Watching Rebecca mother our children blesses my soul with a contentment difficult to describe. Her patience is soft and abundant.

Rebecca: Paul is still my greatest friend, and our level of trust keeps growing as we go through the passages of life. I want to be "for" him and "for" my children. When our second child, a daughter, was born in August 2010, Paul was finishing his last semester of Grad school and I decided it was a great time to potty train our first son. Then the washing machine broke! That fall was probably the most difficult time for me. I was torn between feeling the strain and needing more help, but also wanting dearly to protect Paul's study time so he could reach his graduation goal. After Christmas, things got much easier: I had a washer and dryer and my son was able to do more on his own, including attending to his bathroom needs. I realized that my daughter hated being wet, which had thrown a monkey wrench into her learning how to fall asleep on her own. Finally, Paul had finished all of his course work!

Paul: I will be forever grateful to Rebecca for the load she carried as I was completing my degree. I could see how tired she was at times but never heard her express resentment when I had to bury my head in the books.

Rebecca: We have always had such great family support, especially since we became parents. I am blessed with a deep relationship with my own mother, and a wise mother-in-law who is kind and sensitive enough to share her wisdom when I ask. Both of them have continued eagerly to help me with the children so I have been able to maintain my creative practice, teach other artists, and go out with Paul in the evening for a refresher. I am very sensitive and do not want to overtax the grandparents or bring unruly, overtired children to them. We maintain an afternoon time of rest and a reasonable bedtime hour for the kids in our home. I am so lucky to see how much my children are blessed by spending time with their grandparents. This gives me time and space in my life for adult conversation. Our evenings as a couple are fun times to unwind, have quiet, watch movies, and play. We have such a good time that it's easy to go out if I want an evening with the girls. I always love to get back to Paul. It seems the same for him when he meets his friends for a beer. Our loyalty is still with each other.

Paul: The sexual intimacy and pleasure in our life of 13 years as husband and wife has always been a gift and delight for both of us. When we became pregnant, we searched for ways to keep this precious part of our marriage strong. That was very important to both of us.

Rebecca: Paul has been so sure of this trust in me that I have traveled to foreign countries, stayed with other male artists and friends and spent several weeks apart from him to pursue my work since we have been married, and even since we have had children. The level of trust we have has allowed us to share with each other about sexual temptations we have encountered. There has certainly been opportunity. For me it has never really been a contest: there is still no other man I would rather go to bed with. How could I betray a man so deeply loyal, so deeply affirming, who is such a sensitive lover? What could possibly be better than being close to him? As my pregnancy moved along I got all hung up in my head about my changing body and was less inclined to be in the mood. He was patient, assuring me that we have our whole lives to make love, and that we have enough passion and patience to weather the changes of pregnancy and parenthood.

We were both virgins when we married. I was only 19, feeling clumsy and far from sexy. I was apologetic for my inexperience and he laughed and said, "We have our whole lives to get it right." Always reassuring, Paul has encouraged me, comforted and supported me through these first years of parenthood. People notice how sweet he is with our children and attentive to our needs.

I am still very much in love with him. Of course, we have our moments of irritation, and passion, but reconciling is always quick and deeply desired, as true and loyal friends. It seems awkward to allow unresolved tension between friends, so solving conflicts is now a welcome way through for both of us.

Paul: Rebecca is still the love of my life. She is my comfort and my joy, a place of refuge during stressful days.

Rebecca: I think I have softened since our children arrived, I hope I've become less critical, and more grateful for the work of caring for my family than I ever thought I could be. I have a real sense of being blessed to be with my best friend, and our children, who will one day be grown and gone ... This makes attending dirty diapers, countless meals, aching backs bent over the tub and Cheerios in the floor boards of the car much easier to face. These things don't define me as a person, or us in our marriage. This is just a fleeting passage of our lives that we have been advised by couples who have gone before to savor, share, and enjoy.

Paul: She will always be the sunshine that bursts through my window when I hear her soft laughter and feel her melt in my arms.

Season of Yearning

"In our house, I'm the head...and she's the neck. Everyone knows the neck turns the head wherever it wants to go."

Mr. and Mrs.H.P. Asheville, N.C. Married 18 years

"One word could summarize our marriage and the main reason for it's endurance. That word is commitment. We do not consider divorce an escape, but view tough spells as a time of challenge and perseverance."

Mr. and Mrs.D.P. Charlotte, N.C. Married 16 years

"Blame will poison a marriage; it's a real killer! If you think something she did is 90% of the problem...own the 10%! She will be startled and amazed. It is empowering to do a little light sanding now and then."   Mr. and Mrs. J.D. Boston, MA. Married 18 years

"Leave and cleave. We focus our primary loyalty on each other. Parents will be OK, your Army buddy will make it, her sister is not gonna go bonkers and the kids will survive and be fine if they witness daily the deep endearing love of their parents, year in and year out. It is the greatest gift you can give your children. Your love for each other becomes their rich heritage."

Mr. and Mrs. B.L. Black Mountain, NC Married 47 years

"We taught our children to be respectful. We also taught them to go to bed (bath, story time, night time prayers) and to stay in bed and go to sleep at a decent hour. That gives us some alone time. Don't let the sex fall apart when babies arrive."   Mr. and Mrs. S.O.V. Rochester, N.Y. Married 14 years

Edges of yesterday poke through
the serenity of our morning. . .
shadows of your yesterdays
and mine.
Moments not lived and
memories not loved
dampen the offering
of our outstretched hands.

"And lo, I am with you always
even unto the end of time."

—Matthew 28.:20

Hopes hemmed in longing dash upon rocks
as waves crash toward shore.

The power of unmet expectation exceeded only by
the power of redemptive love.

Staring at the impossible.
No place to go but up,
and nothing to hold onto.

Uncharted territory.
Who will catch me if I fall?

W hen tears
won't stop and
dead ends wander
into dreams....

Blind alleys of
    intention intertwine.

Quagmire of
    circumscribed
    impossibility.

Season of Satisfaction

Part I: Looking Back With Committent

Mike: "Oh what a beautiful morning, oh what a beautiful day." Gordon McRay, his golden voice a memory from long ago – teen years? No before that, I remember as a kid, Mom singing that song – on her good days.

Yes, today is a beautiful morning, sun's been up for a while – still a bit of chill in the fresh mountain air. I love spring! Bette and I get excited each year watching everything we have planted bloom and flower. Color everywhere; a sweet perfume rides on the breeze!

The birds are singing today; I've already stepped out to listen.

I like to ease into my morning cup of coffee, maybe a piece of toast. Some scriptures to start my day off right. Just smelling the clean air, taking a walk. What a blessing. That's enough for me.

Bette: Mike honey, I've got some muffins in the oven. How would you like your eggs?

Mike: Well, if she really would like to know – which she doesn't – it's way too soon to be eating a big breakfast. I've tried to explain this to her, but she likes to start the day together, talking and eating. I guess we are just different. I don't know what to say.

"Okay dear, just over easy is fine.

I'm trying. I really am. This is my third go at marriage and I'm 72. She's 69 and her ex was a real loser, believe me. We are trying so hard to make this work. Some days it's going pretty good.

Then all of a sudden, something will set us off – like throwing a match into a pile of leaves. Boom!

Bette: Are you hungry? Could you make sure the trash is out? Do you want your coffee now?

Mike: Being single for 5 years was kinda nice in a way – on my own timetable, free to do as I pleased, quiet.

Bette: Mike, are you there? I couldn't hear you.

Mike: Oh my God, what does it take? I always remember her birthday with flowers and dinner out. Same for our anniversary – don't never have to be reminded. I know some wives feel the need to drop little hints. Just give me a bit of peace and quiet this time of day. She's in the kitchen, probably about ready to reach for the rollin' pin. Not really, that's just my imagination. I better get in there, I guess. Gotta go.

Bette: Mike, where have you been? Calling you to breakfast shouldn't take so much energy. Like hollering for a lost dog – at least they know how to come for the food whistle!

Mike: Bette, stop. You know I'm not ready for a lot of conversation first thing in the morning. Or a lot of food – neither. I've tried to tell you that – but you don't seem to get it. I try but I get frustrated, and then we're off to a bad start.

Bette: Mike, we both have to be flexible if we are gonna make this work.

Mike: I'm trying – but after 5 years of living alone, it's hard sometimes to give up my old ways.

Bette: I want to start our days out right – make a plan – talk things through. Why don't you ever want to talk with me? Eat a nice hot meal together – that's my vision.

Mike: So we went round and round with this type of thing. Sometimes it got pretty rough, awful uncomfortable. We both had our old habits and our expectations. We were digging ourselves into a pit and at a certain point we realized we needed some help, so we started seeing a marriage counselor together. Got some insight into our dynamics, practiced a few new behaviors. It didn't take hold overnight, but we stuck with it and we practiced together, especially new ways of really listening to each other. Sometimes we would fall back into the blame game and the pity parties. But we caught it sooner with our counselor's expert help, patience and encouragement. We know, now we are gonna make it. We have lots of fun together, lots of shared interests. The big thing is we let the other one be – celebrate our differences. Sometimes it's – "you do your thing and I'll do mine." Some independence, then when we do come together, it's sweet and it's fun.

*For now we see through a glass, darkly;
but then face to face:
now I know in part;
but then shall I know even as also
I am known.*
—1 Corinthians 13:12

Who says you can't teach an old dog new tricks? With a little help from the Lord, a yielded heart, and practice, all things are possible. After twelve years of marriage, Mike and Bette lead the Celebrate Recovery Program at their church and have helped many younger couples learn skills and communication tools in service of a committed marriage.

"Serving God's people is a blessing for us, helping others recommit their lives, and strengthen their marriages and family life. In this way we have been able to give back what we were given."   —Mike & Bette

Seasons

Children Come and Go in Loveliness
In rapture they appear and disappear.

Tender as April's unfolding
They tear love from our imprisoned hopes,
Filling our every day with mystery and music.

Lingering on the doorstep of our hearts
Robed in harvest colors; crimson, orange, gold.

Can it be told, the memories and the dreams?
Spoken softly, whispered in the ear of time,
The meltings we have known,
As moments stretched long into eternity
Wind themselves down drafty corridors and then,
Wind themselves reluctantly back home again.

But celebrate we will their varied orchestrations,
Their wanderings to wintry summits, dancing waves
And turbulent waterfalls of ripe delight.

Still, with open hands we pray
Loosing them to songs that they must sing
And trumphs they must capture,
Pressing footprints into centuries of stone,
Surprising elders with their startling proclamations.

Yes, triumphant they will dance
Stomping their irreverent feet
On stale platitudes constructed to eclipse their hopes
And slow their pulse

All heralded in full array,
Decked for battle they will shout in victory,
Over barren mountains
Through fearsome seas
They will sing their song with passion,
As we applaud from balconies,
Laughter rising on the careless wind.
Our children come and go in loveliness.

Season of Satisfaction

Part II: Looking Back With Pleasure

Ted   She looked radiant. Of course, I had seen the dress before, but tonight was different. Everything about her glowed – her eyes, her skin, her lips felt so incredibly soft. I went dizzy. It was like our very first kiss, the day our passion rose to meet us. During college, after four years of "just friends" the bubble burst and we knew we had fallen in love. Our feelings transformed suddenly, with that first kiss, into a passion, a knowing we were meant for each other, meant to share a life together.

And now tonight, the children, all three little girls, were tucked into bed and sound asleep. It was our "date night" – just the two of us. We did this once a week, planned ahead, sometimes a babysitter and night on the town – catch a movie or even a play. Just us, our special time. But often a date night at home. Something fun and simple for dinner. But always we would dress for each other. Shower, a bit of cologne. Prepared. Every time she would surprise me – rekindle my passion. We would dress separately, I could hardly wait for the surprise of seeing her, standing there – making herself so beautiful – for me! I fell in love with her again, over and over, every week.

Where did she learn all about that, who taught her? I really don't know. I do know her dad loved her mother with a deep profound love. Everyone noticed and as they passed their 63rd wedding anniversary, the children and the grandchildren would ask him: "What is the secret of your long happy marriage?" He would pause and give us the same answer we had all heard before. After a long thoughtful look with his gentle blue eyes, he would say softly, "Choose well. Choose well."

Helen   Yes, Ted and I started out as friends in college. I was dating someone else and Ted would come over occasionally and we would do something fun together. So it was more than just a mandate; "choose well" was a paradigm for me. As a child, I lived that love, basked in that security. Daily I felt the effects of the "choose well" that had enkindled and under-girded my parents' long, happy life together.

Ted   I had the misfortune of enduring the ravages of a happy childhood. *(He chuckles.)* My parents too were happily married. I had a sister and a twin brother. All the families are still close and get together regularly for holidays.

Ted and Helen describe their own childhood and their own marriage as a regular sitcom world. We will dig down to find out how they approach the bumps in the road, but first – how did they meet? Was it electric, passionate chemistry?

Ted   Well, not exactly. In college we were just friends. For the entire four years we each dated other students and then would periodically collide after class and hang out for a while. It was light and fun. We shared interests and began to get to know each other without pretense or expectation.

Helen   I think it is easier that way – being friends first.

Ted   But by grad school neither of us was in a committed relationship and we began to drift closer together.

(Was this a surprise? Candidly, with a little grin, Ted reminisces.)
Well, it was probably in the back of my mind.

Helen   Taking our time was part of choosing well.

Even as the romance heated up it was not incubated in high drama; jealous lovers being left in the dust, gunfights, duels. It was still more "sitcom" than "soap opera" and when their families met the new marriage prospects, both sides were well pleased. Within a year, a wedding was planned. It was a happy, joyous time.

It was another five years before Ted and Helen began having children.

Helen   Before the babies came, any night could be a date night and we had a long while to establish ourselves as husband and wife before the complexities of children demanded our attention and our energy.

Ted   When we became parents there were lots more needs to balance, problems to address and solutions to explore together. Our many years of getting to know each other well had built for us a solid foundation.

Helen   One important thing we learned was how to choose our battles. My anger comes on slowly and takes a long while to burn out. Ted, on the other hand, pops off like a firecracker, says how he feels with lots of energy, and then rolls off over the hills like a thunderstorm. So we recognize our basic differences in that respect and try to accept and understand how we can still be different and yet work it out together.

Don't try to get me over it when I'm still smoldering . . . I need time.

Ted   So we are different in lots of ways; everyone is. What do you do with that? I'll just remake her in my own image. Nice plan. I guess that worked OK for God — maybe not so good for husbands and wives.

Helen   The important thing is to be honest. You let some of the stuff go . . .

but heck, the annoying little habits that are a continual bugaboo, they have to be addressed in an effective and balanced way — the toilet seat, the cap on the toothpaste, the music blaring, the one who is constantly late (even for weddings and funerals!)

Ted   Pick your battles and learn how to let go of some of it. Neither person is going to totally redesign the other — that just ain't gonna happen, now is it honey?

Helen   Nope, not on my watch — when I'm steamed up, you're just gonna have to wait for me to cool down.

Ted   I know honey — it's worth the wait and now that the children are grown — it doesn't happen all that much anymore.

Helen   Once in a blue moon perhaps. If that. *(Laughter.)*

Ted   She's always been a spunky gal. I respect her for that. I admire that quality in my wife — when it doesn't send me off the deep end!

Season of Satisfaction

"Marriage is about compromise. I give a little. She gives a little. . . . Then we do it her way!"

Mr. and Mrs. A.F. Phoenix, AZ. Married 25 years

"We've been married for 7 wonderful years; 18 years actually, but 7 of them have been wonderful."

Mr. and Mrs.T. P. Asheville, N.C. Married 18 years

"The survival of a marriage depends on a good lock at the bedroom door."

Mr. and Mrs. W. C. Sante Fe, N.M. Married 19 years

"When I feel disconnected from her, nothing else in my life seems quite right."

Mr. and Mrs. P. S., Fargo, N.D. Married 10 years

"When we are doing projects together we have developed our own practice. Whoever finishes their chore first, goes over to help the other person with their work until it's done. This is part of how we care for each other every day."

Mr. and Mrs. R.S. Black Mountain, N. C.   Married 27 years

Pastures always greener beyond the footprints of our
well-worn turf.

Longing for new experience and untapped pleasures wrapped
in folly.

I stare at weathered hands, so familiar, to find the thrill in
hands

that cradle memories.

Fields of flowers present distraction
from the mundane flow of
everyday affairs.

To know,
dressed in perfumed ignorance
a lily's innocent delight.

Creator's voice in comfort calls.

The thorn that crowned
the head now decks
the rose.

Into its sleepy serenade
in silence deep
a tune is played
and purpose then
unfolds.

anging on when only time will tell.

For the sport of it we stay
digging in our heels,

to outwit the one
who would betray us to our infidelities.

Season of Challenge
Looking Back With Faith

Bob: *The wind raged and wailed outside of what was left of our home. Determined we huddled together bracing our bodies against the door to our bedroom. Our room of safety and intimacy was now under attack from a hurricane ripping through the Cayman Islands where we had always spent the peaceful winter months. Together, for 5 hours, we struggled to prevent gale force winds gusting up to 210 mph from taking over our last holdout, our final refuge. We knew other parts of our home had already been destroyed.*

What gave us, together as husband and wife, the strength to hold on against such force bent on destroying our home and quite possibly our lives?

Surely, we knew it was the power of God equipping us for this battle and we struggled in constant prayer, knowing deep in our hearts the love of Jesus, his understanding and overpowering all embracing compassion. We quoted scriptures claiming promises from the word of God. We were in our own Garden dealing with the serpent and heard his seductive voice, "Give up, give in, you will never outlast this force." But we heard Moses and the prophets and Christ in the Wilderness going toe to toe with Satan over his lies and temptations. We felt the presence of our Savior and the sweet voice of the Holy Spirit, our Comforter lifting us up, supporting us in our struggle.

Susan: As I bent my knees and pressed my back against the door I thought about our early years together as husband and wife. Three babies in three years called upon all our resources. Living on a farm in Indiana with goats and chickens, there was always lots to do.
As the children grew, they learned how to care for the animals and help in our garden.

Bob: When we married, we knew we were both in it for the long haul. Neither of us considered divorce an option. When things got heavy, throwing in the towel was not our plan B.

Susan: There was no back door to run through when things got too hot in the kitchen. We took our wedding vows very seriously.

Bob: Our priorities were first to God and what we believed He was guiding us to be as a united husband and wife team. Next were our obligations to each other and then to our children. Later, on the list, came our commitments to our work, our family, friends and community.

Susan: It helped immensely to be in a firm agreement together about our priorities and where our commitments were grounded.

We could hear the wind throwing furniture against the other side of the wall. A ripping sound! Was that the roof of the living room being torn off?

I looked now at Bob's face staring down from above. Our eyes met. Here we were in a life and death struggle with the elements. "Are you afraid?" he asked, looking down at my white knuckles pressed against the door frame. "No, not really," I replied. "Maybe a little, but only if I start thinking about it. Let's think about our memories and hope the wind will let up soon."
I remembered the many Thursday nights at 8pm after the babies were in bed, we would have our time together. Fortunately, we had good sleepers so we could count on our evenings alone and review the events of the day.

Bob: That was when we set priorities for the next day and into the week ahead. What did we need, what problems did we want to address together: repairs, bills, to keep the ship afloat?

Susan: In those years, it was basically just keeping everything attended to--children, work, life on a farm. But later, after the kids were grown, I began to feel lonely. For me this became the most difficult season so far in our marriage. By the time we had been married 25 years, I told Bob that I needed more from our relationship. I wasn't threatening divorce. Our marriage was still a sacred covenant for both of us--but something important was missing.

Bob: At first, I didn't really get it – didn't know what she was talking about.

Susan: I had to break it down for him. "I want to be able to really talk with you," I said, "to have intimate conversations where we share our hopes and dreams, worries and sorrows. I need to feel understood."

Do you remember when we went through that?

Bob: Yeah...I heard you finally. I realized we needed some professional help so we could share at a deeper level. Sometimes I felt like you were attacking me – not really listening or letting me explore my own feelings and needs.

Susan: So we did decide to get some help. It meant that much to both of us. This was definitely our season of challenge, and we decided to meet the challenge together...just like we are struggling together today with this terrible hurricane.

Bob: We found a professional couple, therapists in marriage and family, who took us into their home for a whole week, 24 hours a day. They listened to us talk and helped us figure out what was going on and what we could both do to make our communication better and have a deeper, stronger marriage. It was a unique method they had developed. Was it Santa Fe where we went?

Susan: No, it was Alto, New Mexico. They were very skilled. It was amazingly helpful to have two other people watching and listening. They were

able to help us figure out what was going on between us, the dynamics, the meta messages underneath our words.

Bob: *You know what? I think the wind is settling down some. Have you noticed?*

Susan: *Yes, that screeching, howling noise doesn't seem so loud. Do you think we can let go of the door now?*

Bob: *Yes, I think so. You stay here. I'll go take a peek into the living room. Is that okay with you?*

Susan: *If you think it's safe – it does seem like the worst part has finally past.*

Bob: *Okay, I'm gonna go look around.*

Susan: *Be careful – branches might still be falling.*

Bob: *Hey babe – come on out, it looks like we made it!*

Susan: *Oh my God! I can't believe what's out here – total destruction.*

Bob: *Honey, come here. I just want to hold you. I just want to gather you into my arms and never let you go. You were so brave, so strong.*

Look what we did together. We survived!

Susan: *Bob, I'm so glad I married a big guy—a big guy with a big heart. I love you so. Let's pray together. "Thank you Lord God for your protection and your faithfulness."*

Bob: *"Thank you for my beautiful wife...the rose you gave me to love and care for. Thank you, Jesus."*

Season of Challenge

"Marriage is the most challenging, rewarding, frustrating, exhilarating experience imaginable"

Mr. and Mrs. P.S. Fargo, N.D. Married 10 years

"We decided not to fight dirty. We have made a covenant not to insult or tear each other down. After a heated argument, we make up and apologize...forgive...let go. We don't believe in holding grudges overnight and into the next day."

Mr. and Mrs. A.T.B. Black Mountain, N.C. Married 56 years

"Sometimes we just take off! Friends have come to know about the 'privacy factor.' Our marriage comes first. Family has given up on us. We're hopeless. Hopelessly in love!"

Mr. and Mrs. R.N. Norfolk V.A. Married 35 years

"Long suffering is loving someone who makes you suffer—for a long time."

Mr. and Mrs. T. B. Shreveport L.A. Married 36 years

"We each keep a gratitude journal. In the evening we share together what we have been thankful for during the day. This softens our evening, creating intimacy and trust at the end of the day."

Mr. and Mrs. B.M.R. Black Mountain, N.C.   Married 11 years

He: ... "Oh," (he pauses, smiles) "I don't pay her no mind."
She: (tenderly) "Forgive, forgive, forgive."

Mr. and Mrs. J.K. Knoxville, T.N. Married 50 years

"They shall mount up with wings as eagles,
They shall run and not be weary;
They shall walk and not faint."
—Isaiah 40:31

Discovering balance in polarity

Out of step.

Through grace we offer patience past
understanding and love beyond the measure of
our humblest hope.

asting the richness of composted dreams

 A fallen log mothers the tender sprout, green beyond imagining.

Laugher reigns victorious with triumphant shout.

Finding permission to be.
   Like gold hidden in the sandy scrabble of a stream,

   I offer you room to dance with fireflies in summer.

   Twilight's yawning smile returns.

As storms will pass
        rolling off toward restless hills . . .
            . . . words once sharp with edges burning,

knife their way to waters
washed by moonbeam and memories.

My Commitment as a Christian

I'm a part of the fellowship of the unashamed. I have Holy Spirit Power. The die has been cast. I have stepped over the line. The decision has been made. I'm a disciple of His. I won't look back, let up, slow down, back away, or be still.

My past is redeemed, my present makes sense, my future is secure. I'm finished with low living, sight walking, small planning, smooth knees, colorless dreams, tamed visions, mundane talking, cheap living, and dwarfed goals.

I no longer need pre-eminence, prosperity, position, promotions, plaudits, or popularity. I don't have to be right, first, tops, recognized, praised, regarded, or rewarded. I now live by faith, lean on His presence, walk by patience, lift by prayer, and labor by power.

My face set, my gait fast, my goal is heaven, my road is narrow, my way rough, my companions few, my Guide reliable, my mission clear. I cannot be bought, compromised, detoured, lured away, turned back, deluded or delayed. I will not flinch in the face of sacrifice, hesitate in the presence of the adversary, negotiate at the table of the enemy, ponder at the pool of popularity, or meander in the maze of mediocrity.

I won't give up, shut up, let up, until I have stayed up, stored up, prayed up, paid up, preached up for the cause of Christ. I am a disciple of Jesus. I must go till He comes, give till I drop, preach till all know, and work till He stops me. And when He comes for His own, He will have no problems recognizing me—my banner will be clear!

--Written by a young African pastor
and tacked on the wall of his house

Season of Ripeness
Introduction

Finally, through all the years of family drama: children, crises, opportunity, tragedy, joy and fidelity we have arrived at the season of ripeness. Perhaps our association might be an appealing piece of fruit, a melon or a fresh peach. We sniff, we squeeze, wanting to determine if it is ripe. For if it is ripe, we surmise it will be sweet.

A piece of fruit becomes ripe and sweet by absorbing long days of sunshine, good soil and nourishing rainfall. As people formed in God's image, how do we become ripe and sweet? Do some children enter this world with a tender sensitivity for those in need? Do some parents model a desire to serve the Lord along paths particularly arduous and challenging? These attitudes...can they be learned or is it rather God's grace working in the hearts of yielded persons? Perhaps we are all both the suffering hungry heart, and in the same breath, the word of comfort and solace to one in need of patience and compassion. Marriage is work, hard work. The fruit of this endeavor is a pearl of great price.

As we enter into the life of Peter and Birdie Holland, we see a couple in their nineties who have been together for sixty-seven years, married in1945 just before the end of World War II. As lives unfold, sometimes we experience a sense of disappointment, betrayal or tragedy. There is a sweetness in God's mercy as He helps us heal from all life's hurts. In the process He asks something of us — He asks us to forgive. This can often be a very difficult assignment. Sometimes we are afraid to forgive a perpetrator or an enemy, thinking that in some way, to forgive minimizes the offense and our own pain. Or perhaps we believe that to forgive would make us more vulnerable to being hurt again. So we hold onto our grudges, anger, fear, and hatred, as a form of protection. It often seems impossible to move beyond this place of entanglement as we remain trapped in our own fears and limitations. To forgive is to become set free! It is offered through God's unmerited gift of healing grace. By allowing ourselves to be ripened we become a sweet savor to the Father, a sacrificial offering. "Now if we are children, then we are heirs – heirs of God and co-heirs with Christ, if indeed we share in His sufferings in order that we may also share in His glory." (Romans 8:17).

Did Peter and Birdie endure tragedy, pain, or betrayal during their life together? Were they ever falsely accused or unfairly punished? And if so, were they able to find ways to forgive, move forward, embrace the future and leave old hurts behind? What were some of their challenges? Birdie lost her brother Nathan, a soldier during the Allied Invasion at Normandy in the Second World War. She and Nathan had been close and this was a huge and painful grief for Birdie and her entire family, especially her mother. The next tragedy happened after she and Peter were married. Their first child, Sarah, was only two years old when their second daughter, Karen, was born. This precious, tiny child did not live. A deep sorrow took many months to absorb and grieve. Questions like "What if?" and "If only" and "Why me?" kept plaguing Birdie's mind for many months.

Then a year later, the startling news came regarding their plans for a tour of duty together on the mission field in China. Peter would have to go alone – or not at all! Alone as he had been as a child, an only child, craving the company of brothers and sisters. Disappointment. Their dreams of being a mission family in China suddenly were dashed – too dangerous. And later in China, a missionary with his hands tied, witnessing persecution and death. Events Peter described as being etched into his memory as scars are branded onto a steer's hide with hot iron. Atrocities, things he could not talk about. How does a person give all of this to God and move on? Forgiveness, things Peter is still unable to describe; left at the foot of the cross.

Birdie is quiet and sweet, her brown eyes searching my face with a tender compassion. Can she read my eyes also, my disappointments, betrayals, and sorrows? My struggles to forgive? My own failures and victories? I suspect she can. She exudes the wisdom of many years with a generosity of spirit. Birdie seems ready to meet her Savior with patience and a softened heart whenever He calls.

Peter is determined. He has seen much, endured much, and has learned how to do battle with the enemy. His blue eyes convey a confidence, a resolve to be true to the end. He finds his strength and direction in this familiar hymn.

*"Trust and obey,
for there is no other way
to be happy in Jesus
but to trust and obey."*

Season of Ripeness
Looking Back With A Servant's Heart

Peter and Birdie Holland, San Francisco, California, June 1949

Tears whispered down her cheeks as she looked off toward San Francisco Bay and the Golden Gate Bridge shining in the sun. A lovely sight, but for Birdie Holland a sight tinged with a large measure of longing and yes, some deep sadness. His boat slowly became tiny, like a leaf upon a lake. As she felt Sarah by her side and her tiny hand she realized she was clenching it tightly, too tightly perhaps.

"I mustn't let her feel all my emotion. I mustn't trouble her little heart." But when she looked down at her three-year-old daughter, she too was crying for her Papa. Why did it have to be this way? Was it really God's plan, His perfect plan? She was resolved, but now right now, it all felt very heavy. And in her arms baby Dan, a newborn infant felt heavy as well.

"My heart was laden with a mixture of emotion. I was so proud of my husband. Even with a new baby, Peter was willing to take a dangerous mission assignment overseas. Our mission board had at the last minute informed us it would not be safe for me and the children to join Peter in our assignment at South Yunnan Province in China. We were to relieve a missionary couple, Dr. Brown and his wife, who had been in the field for thirty years. Imagine...all their children had been born in China. The Communist Revolution was on the horizon; everyone knew that. Like an approaching storm - the wind was blowing; a heaviness hung in the air. That family certainly deserved a reprieve and Peter did not shirk on his commitment."

Birdie felt her own salty tears and tasted them with her tongue. This would be hard; she knew it would be hard. Even with her mother's help, parenting two young children without Peter's strong presence would be very lonely and difficult at times.

When they received the news from the mission board about the change, they had entered into a period of deep prayer. Together they searched the word of God, seeking the Lord's confirmation and His perfect will. Birdie remembered Peter's words: "When we were told it was too dangerous for Birdie to join me with Sarah and baby Dan, we had to decide together as husband and wife whether I would go alone. What was that discussion like? We prayed together silently and out loud. We honestly shared our feelings together: our fears, worries, excitement, concern. We listened to each other with care. Periods of fasting were commenced to discern God's perfect will. Workers in the mission field like soldiers, police, firemen and first responders are often required to be in very dangerous situations for the service of others. So this was part of what we had signed up for from the very beginning. We had a secure trust in God's protection for those who are called into His service, and we sought guidance in the word of God."

Peter knew he might not live to come back home to his family. The Communists were ruthless in their treatment of their own people. Thousands were slaughtered in public to transform the remainder into terrified submission. Birdie also knew how dangerous it would be for Peter. She knew she would pray for him constantly and she knew, just like the wives of soldiers in battle, he might be asked to make the ultimate sacrifice.

Peter had said, "It was never a consideration for us to go off together and leave the children with family. That was certainly not an option. We were of one mind. After hours of reading the Word and joining together in prayer, our answer came and we were both at peace: *I will never leave you nor forsake you. The Lord is my helper; I will not be afraid* (Hebrews 13:5-6). *I am with you always, even unto the end of time* (Matthew 28:20)."

Birdie joins in, "Yes, that is how the decision was confirmed for us. I committed myself to continue my language study of Chinese in hopes we would be able to join Peter, but we had no idea when that might be."

"And so Mama joined us on this trip to San Francisco. It was such a comfort to have her with us on the train, and she was a great help with the two little children. She understood that I needed this time today to be alone with my family, to say goodbye to Peter and some time to digest it all before she and I caught the train and took the children back to Knoxville, Tennessee, her hometown."

Birdie again let her mind drift back to the day when she and Peter had met. He was at Union Theological Seminary in Richmond, Virginia, and she was pursuing a Master's Degree at Presbyterian School of Christian Education.

Birdie was an athletic girl and had been chosen as a pitcher for the women's softball team. One Saturday Peter had been commandeered to offer his services as an umpire for the ballgame. He could hardly take his eyes off Birdie and was quite impressed by her quick responses and capable handling of the ball.

"Remember," she had confided with a charming little grin, "the pressure was on!"

He asked her out after the game and as he put it: "I was totally sold on Birdie." He continued his courting while he was in Richmond, Virginia, and she was in Asheville, North Carolina. He wrote to her faithfully every day. In their letters they shared their deep Christian faith. Peter knew by then there was a call on his life to be a missionary, and for Birdie, she knew in her heart God was preparing her to be a missionary's wife. The Lord's plan unfolded and by 1945 they had married at First Presbyterian Church in Knoxville, Tennessee, her home church. They wasted no time in beginning their family. It was the year the war ended and it felt like a time of new beginnings. Sarah was born in 1946. A second daughter, Karen, as we remember, was born two years later, and tragedy struck the young family when their beloved baby girl was stillborn. This was a deep sorrow for both parents and it took Birdie many months to work through her grief. Finally in 1949 their first son was born and they named him Dan.

The weather became a bit foggy while Birdie watched Peter's steamer

grow smaller and smaller as it approached the Golden Gate and the open waters of the Pacific. China! She could hardly imagine how far away and how full of danger and uncertainty it was for all missionaries. She glanced at the children, still unwilling to leave her post by the bay. Little baby Dan had dozed off, and Sarah was still gazing out to sea, entranced by the sailboats and seagulls flying above Alcatraz Island. Birdie knew it might be a very long time before she and Peter would be reunited.

Everything was so different after the war ended. Before, everyone saved for the war effort, and many grew their own food in victory gardens. Very few lights were on at night for fear of enemy aircraft. Houses were small and not always well heated. Most people only had iceboxes, not a refrigerator to chill their food. Many folks used the bus, trolley or train since most could not afford automobiles. Gas was rationed and also food. Plastic had not become a staple item of everyday use. Items of daily life were fashioned primarily from wood and iron or glass, copper, brass or steel, as they had been for many centuries. Birdie imagined that the lifestyle in China and energy use there was probably quite primitive. She was sure Peter would have no trouble adapting to all that.

When the mission board had told Peter it would not be safe in China for his wife and two little children, he and Birdie had prayed together and faced this challenging decision united as husband and wife. Birdie had of course felt moments of trepidation at the thought of being alone with their two young children. Peter was concerned about the load he would be putting on his wife if he answered his call alone to the mission field in China. How long might it be before they would allow his family to join him? He did not know.

Birdie found herself reminiscing now about the early years and her own family as a child born in 1920. "My mother called me her little chickadee but my brother Nathan shortened that to 'Birdie'. Now everyone calls me Birdie," she says with a laugh. "I had two brothers and I was in the middle. My older brother was killed in the war. My younger brother, Bob, is 85 and married. They live in Knoxville. My own parents were married in 1916 and had us three children. My father was a county agricultural agent and did experimental work at the University of Tennessee in Knoxville. My mother attended Peabody College in Nashville and got her degree in education and became a teacher before she married my father."

Birdie had a peaceful and happy home life as a child living on the family farm. Everyone sat down for meals together. "It was a very ordered life and we did what our parents told us to do. At breakfast, we all gathered for the same morning menu. Each day this consisted of oatmeal, a soft boiled egg, toast and an orange. You ate it all and washed it down with a glass of milk from the cow. The eggs were from our chickens, and Mama baked our fresh bread two or three times a week. Another theme in our family was simplicity. The food was fresh and wholesome, much of it from our garden and our own animals. Neighbors always shared with each other from their gardens. No preservatives, artificial ingredients or high fructose corn syrup at our table! After breakfast Daddy read from the Bible. We paid attention and listened quietly. We learned about respect, prayer and worship."

"Children in those days were physically active, participated in the daily work of the farm and stayed healthy at a normal weight. They were outdoors in the fresh air much of the day except when they were in class. At recess they had to run around, yell and play, just to stay warm!"

One story that revealed Birdie's character at a very early age included the family bull, Bronco. Birdie loved to play with the young calves, but one day when she was only 4, she found her way into the pasture where Bronco resided. Upon seeing Birdie inside the fence on his territory, the bull charged. With her wits about her, Birdie ran over to a very large oak tree within the fenced pasture. She knew instinctively she could not run fast enough to beat the bull to the fence line. Instead she kept circling the tree, always keeping one step ahead of Bronco who was on the opposite side of the huge tree trunk trying to get to her with his large horns. What a brave and clever little girl! Finally her Daddy saw her plight and raced into the pasture to rescue his tiny daughter. The little Birdie was too quick for the old beast!

Birdie continued to reminisce, not yet wanting to leave the water and head back with the babies. She thought about Peter's early days. He had grown up in Davidson, North Carolina, where his father was on the faculty at Davidson College. Years before, Peter's father had grown up in Montreat, North Carolina, which had been developed in 1903 by Yankees from the North who were trying to build a Christian community there. To this day, Montreat houses a Presbyterian College as well as a Christian Conference Center.

Peter's mother was raised by her aunt and uncle in Texas. She was quite sheltered as a child, but by age 9 she had learned to ride a horse and shoot a rifle.

She practiced hitting targets as she galloped by on her full-sized steed. Peter remained an only child but had a cousin Thomas, 8 years his senior, who became quite like an older brother to the young boy. Occasionally however, Peter was prone to serious nosebleeds, which continued to plague him as he grew older. By 1932, during the great depression, Peter's father took a leave of absence from Davidson College to pursue his doctoral degree. Peter, then age 9, got a taste of what life was like up North.

Finally, dusk was beginning to fall and Birdie decided it was time to head back. Mama might be worrying. It had been a very long day and a sudden weariness descended heavily upon her shoulders. As she trudged along the bay with Sarah at her side, she wondered whether the Chinese officials would allow her husband to write letters home. She could only hope. Hope and pray.

August 1949

My Dearest Birdie,
I think of you every day and you are constantly in my prayers. The trip over went without a hitch and I found Pastor Brown and his family to be well. They were so glad to see me and welcomed me into their home for several weeks before they packed and headed back to the States. They were, I could tell very tired, and ready to head home. Before they left, Pastor Brown helped me make initial contacts with the Chinese Christian Church and its leaders.

I have done some preaching in several churches and soon will begin work with the children who labor in the coal mines. The officials demand our letters be very short. All is well. I send you and Sarah and Dan all my love.

Your devoted husband,
Peter

November 1949

Dearest Birdie,
It has certainly been an adventure so far, my dear. I am now being held at a security police hotel. I have been allowed to work with the young boys who drag coal out of the mines. They are between 8 and 12 years old and have been sold by their families as "slave miners." My heart is extremely heavy, but I must be strong. Recently I have often been confined to a small room. Sometimes they have a Chinese spy stay with me to convince me to give up my Christian faith and embrace the party line. They seem puzzled by my stubborn character. So far their methods have not been extreme, so do not worry. I told them, "You see the evil in a person and want to kill him; we want to change his heart." I know you are in prayer always for me and for those who are suffering here greatly. I love you so and lift you and Sarah and little Dan up to the Lord's tender mercies throughout the day and especially at night. I hope this letter arrives for you. I pray that it does.

Your loving husband, in faith,
Peter

February 1950

My dear wife,

As you know, the situation has changed drastically since the Communists began taking over the country. I am not sure you will get this letter. Life is not so pleasant now and I pray constantly for the local Chinese who have come under heavy persecution. Because of my proficiency in the Chinese language, the officials are suspecting I am a spy. Difficult, but do not worry. All is well. I am still allowed to preach on occasion – but that may not last that much longer. My biggest problem is with my nosebleeds. They have come back worse than ever – perhaps the cold, damp weather.

Your first letter finally arrived. It took 6 months! So wonderful to hear news of you and the children. I love you with all my heart. Our prayers are being heard and answered according to His perfect will and divine timing.

Love as always,

Peter

September 1951

Dear Birdie,

So much has happened since our letters this past year. Everything has now changed drastically under the rule of the Communist Party. My hands are tied in many respects. For me personally there has been an interesting development. As my nose-bleeds progressed and became much worse I began collecting blood in my throat and coughing it up. I could no longer hide this from the guards. They became fearful that I was in the final stages of consumption. In Chinese culture if you die in someone's house it brings a terrible curse upon the family. So now I am a presumed spy ready to die on their doorstep. Not acceptable. I believe they may be making arrangements to have me sent to Hong Kong and then deported. Are you ready to take in an old fella with a bloody nose? I can think of nothing better than to be under your tender, loving care. Seeing Sarah now that she is in school and reading will be such a delight. Your news of the children has meant so much to me, and you are doing such a splendid job. Hearing Dan speaking already in sentences will be exciting.

Please convey my gratitude to your mother for all the help she has provided us during the past several years while I have been gone.

All my love in Jesus Christ,

Peter

Season of Ripeness
Conclusion

Peter was indeed deported from China with a diagnosis of tuberculosis and was sent an exit permit to depart the country from Hong Kong. He left Kunming and embarked on a 3,000 mile trip in a charcoal fired bus. After that he was put on two different boats and transported down the Yangtze River. The last leg of his journey in China was by rail to Hong Kong. He finally arrived in San Francisco in June of 1952 and was greeted by his family. His son, Dan, then age three years old was introduced by Birdie to his father.

She said, "Dan, this is your father."

To which Dan is said to have incredulously replied, "He is not my father. My father is in China!"

In the following two years, the family reunited and returned to Yale Institute of Far Eastern Languages and again studied intensive foreign language – this time Korean. After further preparation Peter, Birdie, Sarah and Dan accepted their first mission assignment together for Korea and flew to Seoul in June 1954. Their second son, Timothy was born in Seoul on December 7, 1954, a year and four months after the Armistice was signed, July 27, 1953.

The family remained in Korea until 1964 working with peasants and helping to grow the Christian Church for ten years after the Korean War.

AFTER KATRINA
. . . and Rwanda, Haiti, Fukushima Daiichi and . . . .

A drawing based on a newspaper photograph of a man with his wife and child after they lost their home in the flood. His tender care reminded Sophia of Jesus and all the children Jesus loves.

". . . and a little child will lead them." —Isaiah 11:6

Season of Ripeness

"When I was a little boy I learned to tie my shoe. On occasion I needed somebody to help me undo the knots. Same in marriage. Could be a priest, a counselor, somebody neutral with experience. The knots can be tricky." Mr. and Mrs. R.S. Troy, N.Y. Married 58 years

"Every morning and every evening I take my wife in my arms and we embrace each other. Then we each offer a special blessing over the one we love. We pray these blessings every day...no matter what. If we are not together, we bless each other over the telephone." Mr. and Mrs. D. H. Black Mountain, N.C. Married 20 years

"To have the opportunity to know another and be known by another—with all our doubts, fears, and failures—is perhaps the greatest gift life offers." Mr. and Mrs. F.S Toledo, Ohio Married 30 years

"Marriage is more than compromise. You give all you can and hope he gives all he can. Then you pray, with God's help, it will be enough to keep the marriage together." Mr. and Mrs.H.S. Asheville, N.C. Married 53 years

"In tight spots, she says, 'No big deal.' Then I say, 'This is true.'" Mr. and Mrs.T.B. Shieveport, L.A. Married 46 years

To a place of surrender
we arrive with suits of armor
melted in the blazing sun.

Burned and broken till only the
marrow of our bones
cries out in victory.

Heated in refiner's fire,
    finest vein of purest gold remains.

        Sweet chariot of hope
    carries the dross apart,
testimony
        to a faithful lover's heart.

Cinders still warm
celebrate an eerie incandescence.

Courageous shoots of green sprout
forth through ashes on a barren hill.

Triumphant purpose barks
in early morning mist.
Commitment is renewed and
digs itself a roothold
singing to the blackened earth . . .

the blackened earth.

To stand together in the opulence of arid times, withered and wrinkled. Remembering lullabies and nursery rhymes.

Childhood comes round again to haunt us with its dreamy reverie.

Witness to a Walk of Sixty Years
…upon observing roses resting on the surface of Lake Susan

Were it possible
    there could be a love so large
so enduring
    so sweet and deep and brave
    so unmistakable

that she could see
    from her vantage beyond the sky
      high above spring daffodils
    daring in mid-March to bloom

    high above, tender maple blossoms
red in their ebullient inundation
    against a cobalt sky

above patchwork clouds
    above, above and beyond it all

that she could see and know,
    with certainty that you remember.

That you remember
    the holding of hands,
the ring you slipped upon her finger
The sacrament of a first kiss
    of clear lake water
reflecting back in the depth of her dark eyes
    the promise of hope
    of love, of a life together.

As it turned out, a long life.
    A gift not always given
      not always received
    recognized or cherished:
three score years.

But to remember this journey you now come
    to honor,not from duty nor from obligation
      but from the heart.

You have arrived
    taking in the familiar scene;
    the lake, the dam, the forest in early spring.
You have come for purpose,
    to leave a gift, to cast your roses.

Alone, a huge white swan gliding past
    did not comprehend.
Was it food you tossed?
Was he defending his territory
    (as was his wont on most occasions)
not feeling at all obliged nor disposed
    to allow you
    the felicity of your own tender dreams?

Not deterred by an irascible old bird
    you stake out your claim
    in this prescient place
    that captured such meaning
    held such promise, such hope
    so many, long years ago.
And through those years
    words echo back
    bouncing off the corridors
    of your crowded thought.
"Forgive me, as I forgive you
    for moments of self-absorption
    generosity not extended,
    words not well chosen
moments of neglect."

"For anger and fear
    for blood, sweat and tears
    for weary years and trying years
    and years that tore our hearts.
        Years of healing and repair
           Years of hunger for fresh air."

"Time to face the challenge of two,
    or three or four or more. Ups and downs
Whirling round, clowns.
      Who are you? Who am I?
      Spinning on the ice in arabesque."

"Time to listen well, and to be still,
    to find our center and our truth."

"A radical truth that fits perfectly
    in the particular space between
      your voice and mine.
Notes bring harmony
    when discord threatens."
A mitered joint fitted
    must be cut and smoothed
      with sand and grit.
Marriage is not for timid folk
    nor faint of heart.
Marriage is not intended
    to be a perfect weave;
a spectator sport with
blue ribbons and golden cups.

Magnificence of design manifests
beyond the lumps, tangles lost stitches
    and bumps in the road. A marathon.
    Are you still standing at the end?
Do you cross the line together?

Yes, from her vantage she sees now
    because her heart knew then,
      how deep and wide was that love,
enduring through years and seasons
    maple trees and daffodils, red bud,
      forsythia, trillium - a sapphire lake
strewn with long stemmed roses,
    bright as yellow sunshine, they dapple
    and dance upon the rippled water.

—Sophia V. Brooks

"I pray that you, being rooted and established in love, may have strength, together with all the saints, to grasp how wide and long and high and deep is the love of Christ, and to know this love that surpasses knowledge – that you may be filled to the measure of all the fullness of God."

- Ephesians 3:14-21

Home is where the hearth is

Photo Credits

ABOUT THE GUEST PHOTOGRAPHERS:

Joe & Monica Cook: *Both Atlanta natives and Appalachian Trail hikers, Joe and Monica Cook also work as freelance photographers and writers who share their lifochrome photographic prints from the famous 2,000-mile footpath at art shows throughout the Eastern US. www.joecook.net*

Steven David: *Located in Marietta, Georgia, Steven is known for his nature photography. He presents his work at shows throughout the Southeast where the author found this incredible photo of an eagle, a dramatic addition to her book. www.stevendavid.com*

J. Scott Graham: *Since 1990, J. Scott Graham's award winning photography has gained national recognition by demonstrating an artistic viewpoint and revealing a unique ability to bring fresh focus to a familiar subject. www.jscottgraham.com*

Alan Ostmann: *Alan's love of photography began in the years of the Kodak Brownie and has continued into the present digital age. His philosophy of life and photography is: what we respect and love unconditionally, will reveal its true self. Living this philosophy is how he captures the many facets of beauty in nature. www.ileaveonlyfootsteps.com*

Jennifer Pickering: *Jennifer is a documentary photographer, music lover, and world traveler. Through a nonprofit international music festival, Lake Eden Arts Festival (LEAF), Jennifer has engaged performers & mentors to bring music education, performance, and instruments into the lives of under served children in North Carolina and beyond. www.jenpickering.com*

Stephen A. Snider: *For many years Dr. Stephen Snider, DC has served the Asheville, NC community as a skilled chiropractor. He is also a rugged outdoorsman, fisherman and nature photographer. The pictures he has graciously contributed were taken in the Rocky Mountains.*

Visio Photography: *A husband and wife team, James and Jen, who love people and art and feel that photography is the perfect medium for them to express their passion. To see more of their work, please visit www.visiophotography.com.*

ABOUT THE AUTHOR:

Sophia V. Brooks farms in the mountains of Western North Carolina where many of these photographs were taken. She still prefers shooting film in her clasic Pentax and cooks on a wood stove. She knows from personal experience the painful cost of divorce on children, adults and the entire fabric of our society. Events in her life, including her parents' divorce when she was a child and the break up of her own marriage, led her to discover the saving love of Jesus Christ in the winter of 1972. Through His transforming grace and empowerment, she developed a deep commitment to help married couples strengthen and maintain their marriages. She is in private practice as a Licensed Marriage and Family Therapist in Black Mountain, North Carolina. The name of her business is ***Families: A Renewable Resource***. It is her hope that this book will be an inspiration and encouragement to many people.

(You may contact the author through the publisher: www.spiritofappalachia.org)

The Lord is my Rock and my Fortress . . . .
—Psalms 18:2